Erin Strakalaitis

D1737328

NOBODY'S
looking at you

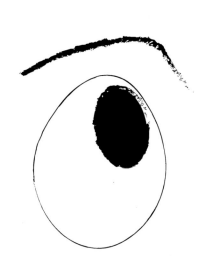
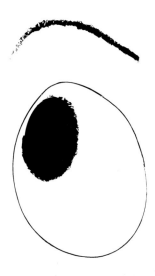

Joyfulness can be
found in any situation.

Erin

THIS IS
A BOOK
ABOUT

NOBODY

THIS IS
NOBODY

HE'S A BIT SHY

could you introduce
yourself to him?

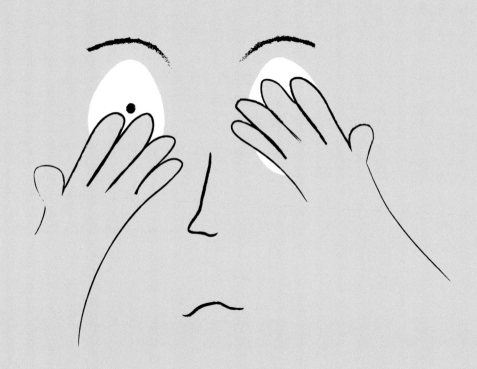

MAYBE

he would feel better
if you said your name
with a silly voice!

IT WORKED!
GREAT JOB!

i think he finds
you funny.

hmmm. . . i wonder. . .

. . . what else you could do

when nobody's **LOOKING** at you...

WOULD YOU

make your
silliest face?

or WOULD YOU

perform a drum solo
when nobody's around?

WHAT IF

we count to three
and play hide & seek?

1. . .

2...

3...

nobody is
nowhere
to be found!

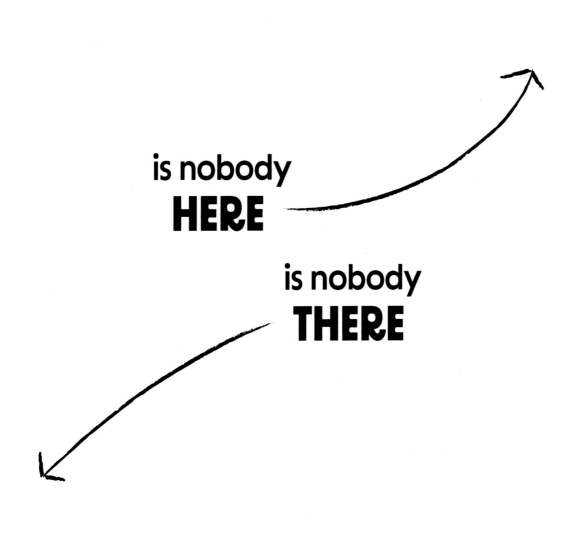

is nobody
HERE

is nobody
THERE

maybe if we
sing a silly song
nobody will appear.

READY?

Deee Daa DOOoo
noddi noddi BOO BOO
where'd NOBODY go to?
Marr MaRR SUPERSTAR
show me where nobody
ArrrrreeE

PHEW!

there he is!

COULD YOU

pretend to splash
in puddles and
dance in the rain?

OOPS. . .

maybe we should
dry him off?

SHAKE! SHAKE! SHAKE!

WELL. . .

at least he's dry now!

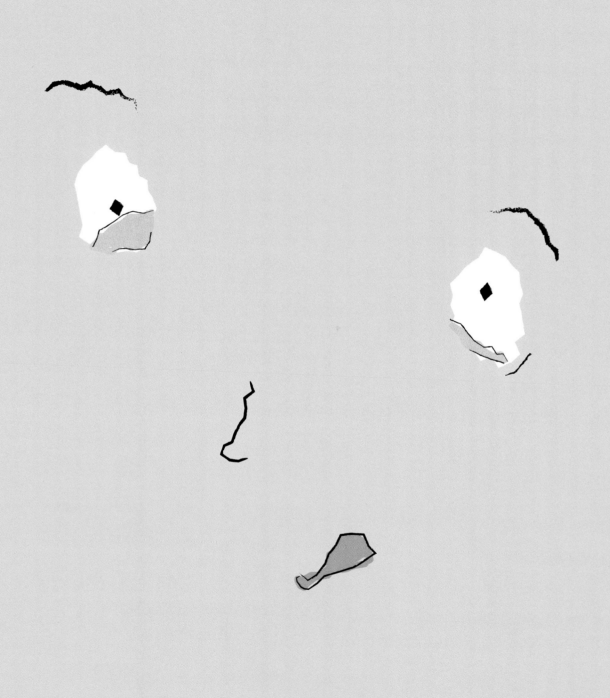

i think we
tired him out.

but before you go...

PLEASE

KNOW

there is always a
silly thing to do...

when nobody's
looking at you!

Made in the USA
Monee, IL
05 May 2024